The Poetry of Protest    821.008

**Hertfordshire**
COUNTY COUNCIL
Libraries, Arts
& Information

**Please return this book
on or before the last
date shown or ask for i'
to be renewed.**

L 32

Please renew/return this item by the last date shown.

So that your telephone call is charged at local rate,
please call the numbers as set out below:

|  | From Area codes 01923 or 0208: | From the rest of Herts: |
|---|---|---|
| Renewals: | 01923 471373 | 01438 737373 |
| Enquiries: | 01923 471333 | 01438 737333 |
| Minicom: | 01923 471599 | 01438 737599 |

L32b

edited by Simon Fuller

BBC/LONGMAN

# Introduction

Poetry and protest go well together. In some situations, the act of writing is itself a protest. In others, protest is only possible through the limited exploitation of a piece of paper and a pencil. Poetry is by nature subversive. By its style and form it challenges our preconceptions of language, and in turn, our thinking and understanding. It is an ideal medium for confronting injustice, inequality and indifference.

This is not essentially a book of hard-hitting haikus or reinforced steel sonnets. It is intended as a varied and wide-ranging selection of poems especially suitable for study at GCSE or Standard Grade. There is a historical strand to the selection and a cross-cultural one. Protest is apparently timeless and universal, which is good news.

Many of these poems were selected for a BBC radio series, called 'The Poetry of Protest', first broadcast in September 1991 on Radio 5. I should like to thank the following for their invaluable guidance in making that original selection: Gillian Allnutt for Women's Voices; Fred D'Aguiar for Black Voices; Mike Rosen for Workers' Voices; Jane Sherwin for Prisoners' Voices and Colin Smith, the producer of the radio programmes.

'We care about texts for many reasons, not the least of which is that they bring us news that alters our way of interpreting things. If this were not the case, the Gospels and the teachings of Karl Marx would have fallen upon deaf ears. Textual power is ultimately power to change the world.'

Robert Scholes, *Textual Power*

# Contents

# *Black* VOICES

## *Workers'* VOICES 56

## Prisoners' VOICES

82

# Youth VOICES

**\* denotes poems on accompanying cassette**

# Women's
# VOICES

As we know women have been writing poetry for as long as men, but it is amazing how many poetry anthologies ignore this. Aphra Benn wrote protest poetry in the seventeenth century and lived as a professional writer, but how many know of her writings?

It isn't that women's poetry is essentially different from men's, but that it has been so consistently ignored in the past. Now, there might be a danger that women's poetry is placed in a ghetto and separated from the mainstream. And although this section of the book is specifically written by them, women poets do appear in all the other sections of the book also.

In recent times women's protest has often been portrayed as anti-men. Some of it has been, and with good reason. But women have plenty of concerns other than men and their poetry reflects this. Some poetry here, from Liz Lochhead or Wendy Cope, is about men and male attitudes. Other poetry here is about global issues such as the environment, animal rights, war – nuclear and conventional, old age, betrayal and intrusion into personal life. At the end of the section, Emily Brontë and Grace Nichols insist on the right to be women, on their own terms.

# Men Talk (Rap)

## Liz Lochhead

Women
Rabbit rabbit rabbit women
Tattle and titter
Women prattle
Women waffle and witter

Men Talk. Men Talk.

Woman into Girl Talk
About Women's trouble
Trivia 'n' Small Talk
They yap and they babble

Men Talk. Men Talk.

Women yatter
Women chatter
Women show the fat, women spill the beans
Women aint been takin'
The oh-so Good Advice in them
Women's Magazines.

A Man likes A Good Listener.

Oh yeah
I like A Woman
Who likes me enough
Not to nitpick
Not to nag and
Not to interrupt 'cause I call that treason
A woman with the Good Grace
To be struck dumb
By me Sweet Reason. Yes —

A Man likes a Good Listener

A Real
Man
Likes a Real Good Listener

Women yap yap yap
Verbal Diarrhoea is a Female Disease
Woman she spread she rumours round she
Like Philadelphia Cream Cheese.

Oh
Bossy Women Gossip
Girlish Women Giggle
Women natter, women nag
women niggle niggle niggle

Men Talk.

Men
Think First, Speak Later
Men Talk.

# Rondeau Redoublé

*Wendy Cope*

There are so many kinds of awful men –
One can't avoid them all. She often said
She'd never make the same mistake again:
She always made a new mistake instead.

The chinless type who made her feel ill-bred;
The practised charmer, less than charming when
He talked about the wife and kids and fled –
There are so many kinds of awful men.

The half-crazed hippy, deeply into Zen,
Whose cryptic homilies she came to dread;
The fervant youth who worshipped Tony Benn –
'One can't avoid them all,' she often said.

The ageing banker, rich and overfed,
Who held forth on the dollar and the yen –
Though there were many more mistakes ahead,
She'd never make the same mistake again.

The budding poet, scribbling in his den
Odes not to her but to his pussy, Fred;
The drunk who fell asleep at nine or ten –
She always made a new mistake instead.

And so the gambler was at least unwed
And didn't preach or sneer or wield a pen
Or hoard his wealth or take the Scotch to bed.
She'd lived and learned and lived and learned but then
There are so many kinds.

# XWORDS

*Janice Galloway*


you tokinti me?
you tokinti
scuse ma french amean
words urny ma forte but
if yi dont mind me sayin
no meanin this cheeky like but
ifyi take ma tip
take ma advice
ifyi want ma HONEST opinion
SON
uv what a thinkiv yir
PATHETIC proposition ti a
grownup wumman that kid
CHEWYI uppan SPITyi
withoot thi bothiruv
puttinur TEETH in

see what ad DO son
what ad DO
is bifore a loss thi rag COMPLETELY yill
rearrange these words intia
wellknown phrase ur sayin

before a beat yur CLOCK in.

# Man Monologue

*Liz Lochhead*

Men says My Boss
are definitely more dependable
and though even in these days of equal pay
men tend to come a wee bitty more expensive
due to the added responsibility a man tends to have
in his job specification
Well for instance you can depend on a man not to get
pregnant.
My Boss says men are more objective.
Catch a man bitching
about health hazards and conditions
and going on strike over no papertowels in the toilet
or nagging over the lack of day nursery facilities
My Boss says as far as he's concerned a crèche is a motor
    accident in Kelvinside
and any self respecting woman should have a good man
to take care of her so it's only pinmoney anyway
and that's bound to come out in the attitude.
Well a man isn't subject to moods
or premenstrual tension a guy
isn't going to phone in sick with some crap about cramps.
My Boss says a man rings in
with an upset stomach and you know either
he means a hangover or else his brother
managed to get him a ticket for Wembley.

You know where you are with a man.

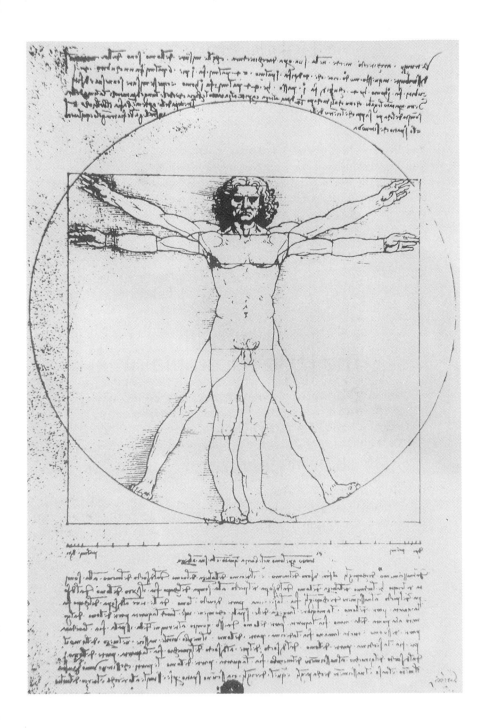

# Lightly Bound

*Stevie Smith*

You beastly child, I wish I had miscarried,
You beastly husband, I wish I had never married.
You hear the north wind riding fast past the window? He calls me.
Do you suppose I shall stay when I can go so easily?


*from:*

# The Wife's Complaint

*Anonymous*


Our lips had smiled to swear hourly
that nothing should split us – save dying –
nothing else. All that has changed:
it is now as if it never had been,
our friendship. I feel in the wind
that the man dearest to me detests me.
I was banished to this knoll knotted by woods
to live in a den dug beneath an oak.
Old is this earthen room; it eats at my heart.

May grief and bitterness blast the mind
of that young man! May his mind ache
behind his smiling face! May a flock of sorrows
choke his chest! He would change his tune
if he lived alone in a land of exile
far from his folk.

# The Dolphins

*Carol Ann Duffy*

World is what you swim in, or dance, it is simple.
We are in our element but we are not free.
Outside this world you cannot breathe for long.
The other has my shape. The other's movement
forms my thoughts. And also mine. There is a man
and there are hoops. There is a constant flowing guilt.

We have found no truth in these waters,
no explanations tremble on our flesh.
We were blessed and now we are not blessed.
After travelling such space for days we began
to translate. It was the same space. It is
the same space always and above it is the man.

And now we are no longer blessed, for the world
will not deepen to dream in. The other knows
and out of love reflects me for myself.
We see our silver skin flash by like memory
of somewhere else. There is a coloured ball
we have to balance till the man has disappeared.

The moon has disappeared. We circle well-worn grooves
of water on a single note. Music of loss forever
from the other's heart which turns my own to stone.
There is a plastic toy. There is no hope. We sink
to the limits of this pool until the whistle blows.
There is a man and our mind knows we will die here.

# Two Sketches

*Gillian Allnutt*

## Hiroshima, 1945

Kasa promises. She walks
carefully all the way back
from the shop.

She has one foot on the step
when the sun slips. Her shadow stops.
She looks up.

The sun
does not fall down
until late in the afternoon.

That is a promise. It has been
given to us.
It is only eight fifteen.

She is bringing a bottle of rice wine.
It is precious.
There will be a celebration.

The house is gone.
Kasa stops. There is a shadow on the step
looking up.

# Birmingham, 1983

Alice examines the shadow
that lies before her
like a future.

It is fantastic:
an elegant woman dressed in black,
an old one bent over a stick.

Alice stops short.
She is only eight,
but she can just imagine it.

Alice, come on up.
The sun has reached the bottom of the step.
It is quarter past eight.

Tomorrow is
another day. That is a promise.
Come.

Alice forgets her shadow. Carelessly
it hops before her
two steps at a time.

# I Coming Back

*Grace Nichols*

I coming back 'Massa'
I coming back

mistress of the underworld
I coming back

colour and shape
of all that is evil
I coming back

dog howling outside
yuh window
I coming back

ball-of-fire
and skinless higue
I coming back

hiss in yuh ear
and prick in yuh skin
I coming back

bone in yuh throat
and laugh in yuh skull
I coming back

I coming back 'Massa'
I coming back

# Bipeds, Beware

*Hazel Archard*

*(Insects may well have the last laugh, but perhaps we can still smile)*
Before you put
your upstart foot
upon a millipede
remember he
has pedigree:
Respect an ancient breed
that scrambled free
from ancient sea
to nibble ancient weed.
He did not learn
to blast and burn
nor bare his gums to bleed;
mild herbivore,
he asks no more
than may fulfil his need.
Along the edge
of softish veg
he finds his frugal feed,
and once replete
he shifts his feet.
(The front ones take the lead.)
He would not rate
our Heads of State
remotely fit to plead
who aim to fry
all earth and sky
to keep our corpses freed.
This little lowly
roly poly
holds to a peaceful creed;
he bends his knees
(a lot of these!)
and tells a passing bead
to Arthropod

his guardian god,
segmented, multi-kneed,
most wise and just
from foot to crust
in heart and mind and deed.
O, bipeds who
have just come through,
all thrusting strength and speed,
whose flailing arm
does mostly harm,
who stride in lust and greed.
Admire the ways
of one whose days
are very long indeed!

# Written after Hearing about the Soviet Invasion of Afghanistan

*Sujata Bhatt*

Here,
a child born
in winter
rarely survives.
Bibi Jamal's son died.
She pounds hard dough,
kneads in yak milk, quickly kneads in fat,
rolls the dough out round and flat.
Her older co-wife cooks the bread.
Bibi Jamal can't speak of it yet.

It's cold enough. Birds have come inside.
Her co-wife sleeps, thick feet
by the fire in the yurt's centre.
On the fire's other side Bibi Jamal weaves
diagrams of Darjeeling into a carpet:
Hills sprouting tea-leaves, rivers in froth down mountains,
and there must be red, she feels,
red skirts flowing through fields,
ripe pomegranates broken open in some garden.
With such green
with such blue Himalayan sky
there's always red.

Nothing like
the granite, treeless
mountains she knows.

Bibi Jamal's thread never breaks,
even as she dreams of Darjeeling.
And her husband, already on the Hindu Kush,
doesn't know how her breasts ache with milk.

She can include
his voice slicing through miserable gusts;
caravanserai well-water strawberry on his tongue.
So, she listens: snow visits,
her husband pitches his black tent.
She spots nearby
a slouched snow-leopard.
It moves, makes her jump,
stops for a minute, noses the air, steals
away through sharp sword grass.
Her husband remains
safe in his black tent.
He'll be beyond the Khyber pass soon.
She draws green thread through her fingers.

What do you know of Bibi Jamal?
Her husband, napalmed,
ran burning across the rocks.
Crisp shreds of skin, a piece of his turban,
a piece of his skull were delivered to her.
She only stared, didn't understand,
muttered, 'Allah Allah Allah Allah is great. But,
where is my husband? Allah Allah Allah.'
She'll ask you when she understands.

# The Telephone Call

## Fleur Adcock

They asked me 'Are you sitting down?
Right? This is Universal Lotteries',
they said. 'You've won the top prize,
the Ultra-super Global Special.
What would you do with a million pounds?
Or, actually, with more than a million –
not that it makes a lot of difference
once you're a millionaire.' And they laughed.

'Are you OK?' they asked – 'Still there?
Come on, now, tell us, how does it feel?'
I said 'I just . . . I can't believe it!'
They said 'That's what they all say.
What else? Go on, tell us about it.'
I said 'I feel the top of my head
has floated off, out through the window,
revolving like a flying saucer.'

'That's unusual' they said. 'Go on.'
I said 'I'm finding it hard to talk.
My throat's gone dry, my nose is tingling.
I think I'm going to sneeze – or cry.'
'That's right' they said, 'don't be ashamed
of giving way to your emotions.
It isn't every day you hear
you're going to get a million pounds.

Relax, now, have a little cry;
we'll give you a moment . . .' 'Hang on!' I said.
'I haven't bought a lottery ticket
for years and years. And what did you say
the company's called?' They laughed again.
'Not to worry about a ticket.
We're Universal. We operate
a Retrospective Chances Module.

Nearly everyone's bought a ticket
in some lottery or another,
once at least. We buy up the files,
feed the names into our computer,
and see who the lucky person is.'
'Well, that's incredible' I said.
'It's marvellous. I still can't quite . . .
I'll believe it when I see the cheque.'

'Oh,' they said, 'there's no cheque.'
'But the money?' 'We don't deal in money.
Experiences are what we deal in.
You've had a great experience, right?
Exciting? Something you'll remember?
That's your prize. So congratulations
from all of us at Universal.
Have a nice day!' And the line went dead.

# The Caged Bird

*Emily Brontë*

And like myself lone, wholly lone,
It sees the day's long sunshine glow;
And like myself it makes its moan
In unexhausted woe.

Give we the hills our equal prayer:
Earth's breezy hills and heaven's blue sea;
We ask for nothing further here
But our own hearts and liberty.

Ah! Could my hand unlock its chain,
How gladly would I watch it soar,
And ne'er regret and ne'er complain
To see its shining eyes no more.

But let me think that if to-day
It pines in cold captivity,
To-morrow both shall soar away
Eternally, entirely Free.

# Holding My Beads

*Grace Nichols*

Unforgiving as the course of justice
Inerasable as my scars and fate
I am here
a woman . . . with all my lives
strung out like beads before me

It isn't privilege or pity
that I seek
It isn't reverence or safety
quick happiness or purity but

the power to be what I am/a woman
charting my own futures/a woman
holding my beads in my hand

# Black

# VOICES

Black poetry is concerned with as wide a range of issues as any other, but it is inevitable that the racism that has dominated so much of black people's experience should be represented here, as well as poetry about the environment, sexism, religion and so forth.

There is a variety in tone and style and you will notice the variation in spelling. The spelling reflects the accent and guides the pronunciation. Most of the poetry is written in Standard English but the reader will notice examples of creole, such as 'fi' and 'we dads'. The poetry challenges prejudices towards black language, amongst other things, as explored in John Agard's 'Listen Mr Oxford Don'.

Some poems are tough and uncompromising, some are quiet and reflective. They are all, in their way, are a celebration of the power of language to express opposition, to set a new agenda. Very importantly, many of the poets represented here make live and lively performances of their work and have contributed immeasurably to a revitalisation of poetry in the last decade.

As with women's poetry, there is a danger that a section like this separates black poetry off into another ghetto. In fact, black writers are represented in every section of this anthology, but uniquely so in this one.

# Colonisation in Reverse

*Louise Bennett*

Wat a joyful news, Miss Mattie,
I feel like me heart gwine burs'
Jamaica people colonizin
Englan in reverse.

By de hundred, by de t'ousan
From country and from town,
By de ship-load, by de plane-load
Jamaica is Englan boun.

Dem a-pour out o' Jamaica,
Everybody future plan
Is fe get a big-time job
An settle in de mother lan.

What an islan! What a people!
Man an woman, old and young
Jusa pack dem bag an baggage
An tun history upside dung!

Some people don't like travel,
But fe show dem loyalty
Dem all a-open up cheap-fare-
To-Englan agency.

An week by week dem shippin off
Dem countryman like fire,
Fe immigrate an populate
De seat o' de Empire.

Oonoo see how life is funny,
Oonoo see de tunabout,
Jamaica live fe box bread
Outa English people mout'.

For wen dem catch a Englan,
An start play dem different role,
Some will settle down to work
An some will settle fe de dole.

Jane say de dole is not too bad
Because dey payin she
Two pounds a week fe seek a job
Dat suit her dignity.

Me say Jane will never find work
At the rate how she dah look,
For all she stay pon Aunt Fan couch
An read love-story book.

What a devilment a Englan!
Dem face war an brave de worse,
But I'm wonderin how dem gwine stan
Colonizin in reverse.

# Telephone Conversation

*Wole Soyinka*

The price seemed reasonable, location
Indifferent. The landlady swore she lived
Off premises. Nothing remained
But self-confession. 'Madam,' I warned,
'I hate a wasted journey – I am African.'
Silence. Silenced transmission of
Pressurized good-breeding. Voice, when it came,
Lipstick coated, long gold-rolled
Cigarette-holder pipped. Caught I was, foully.
'HOW DARK?' . . . I had not misheard . . . 'ARE YOU LIGHT
OR VERY DARK?' Button B. Button A. Stench
Of rancid breath of public hide-and-speak.
Red booth. Red pillar-box. Red double-tiered
Omnibus squelching tar. It *was* real! Shamed
By ill-mannered silence, surrender
Pushed dumbfoundment to beg simplification.
Considerate she was, varying the emphasis –
'ARE YOU DARK? OR VERY LIGHT?' Revelation came.
'You mean – like plain or milk chocolate?'
Her assent was clinical, crushing in its light
Impersonality. Rapidly, wave-length adjusted,
I chose. 'West African sepia' – and as afterthought,
'Down in my passport.' Silence for spectroscopic
Flight of fancy, till truthfulness clanged her accent
Hard on the mouthpiece. 'WHAT'S THAT?' conceding
'DON'T KNOW WHAT THAT IS.' 'Like brunette.'
'THAT'S DARK, ISN'T IT?' 'Not altogether.
Facially I am brunette, but, madam, you should see
The rest of me. Palm of my hand, soles of my feet
Are a peroxide blond. Friction, caused –
Foolishly, madam – by sitting down, has turned
My bottom raven black – One moment, madam!' – sensing
Her receiver rearing on the thunderclap
About my ears – 'Madam,' I pleaded, 'wouldn't you rather
See for yourself?'

# Half-caste

*John Agard*

Excuse me
standing on one leg
I'm half-caste

Explain yuself
wha yu mean
when yu say half-caste
yu mean when picasso
mix red an green
is a half-caste canvas/
explain yuself
wha yu mean
when yu say half-caste
yu mean when light an shadow
mix in de sky
is a half-caste weather/
well in dat case
england weather
nearly always half-caste
in fact some o dem cloud
half-caste till dem overcast
so spiteful dem dont want de sun pass
ah rass/
explain yuself
wha yu mean
when yu say half-caste
yu mean tchaikovsky
sit down at dah piano
an mix a black key

wid a white key
is a half-caste symphony/

Explain yuself
wha yu mean
Ah listening to yu wid de keen
half of mih ear
Ah looking at yu wid de keen

half of mih eye
an when I'm introduced to yu
I'm sure you'll understand
why I offer yu half-a-hand
an when I sleep at night
I close half-a-eye
consequently when I dream
I dream half-a-dream
an when moon begin to glow
I half-caste human being
cast half-a-shadow
but yu must come back tomorrow

wid de whole of yu eye
an de whole of yu ear
an de whole of yu mind

an I will tell yu
de other half
of my story

# Di Great Insohreckshan

## Linton Kwesi Johnson

it woz in April nineteen eighty-wan
doun inna di ghetto af Brixtan
dat di babylan dem cause such a frickshan
an it bring about a great insohreckshan
an it spread all ovah di naeshan
it woz a truly an historical okayjan

it woz event af di year
an I wish I ad been dere
wen wi run riot all ovah Brixtan
wen wi mash-up plenty police van
wen wi mash-up di wicked wan plan
wen wi mash-up di Swamp Eighty-wan
fi wha?
fi mek di rulah dem andahstan
dat wi naw tek noh more a dem oppreshan

an wen mi check out
di ghetto grapevine
fi fine out all I coulda fine
evry rebel jussa revel in dem story
dem a taak bout di powah an di glory
dem a taak bout di burnin an di lootin
dem a taak bout smashin an di grabbin
dem a tell mi bout di vanquish an di victri

dem seh: di babylan dem went too far
soh wha?
wi ad woz fi bun two kyar
an wan an two innocent get mar
but wha?
noh soh it goh sometime inna war
een star
noh soh it goh sometime inna war?

dem seh: win bun dung di George
wi coulda bun di lanlaad
wi bun dung di George
wi nevah bun di lanlaad
wen wi run riot all ovah Brixtan
wen wi mash-up plenty police van
wen wi mash-up di wicked wan plan
wen wi mash-up di Swamp Eighty-wan

dem seh: we commandeer kyar
an wi ghaddah aminishan
wi buil wi barricade
an di wicked ketch afraid
wi sen out wi scout
fi goh fine dem whereabout
den wi faam-up wi passi
an wi mek wi raid

now dem run gaan
goh plan countah-hackshan
but di plastic bullit
an di waatah canon
will bring a blam-blam
will bring a blam-blam
nevah mine Scarman
will bring a blam-blam

# Nothing Said

*Brenda Agard*

We marched half the day
Until our feet were sore
Until the pain goes away
We will march some more

What do we want?
JUSTICE
When do we want it?
NOW

We felt for our
sisters and our brothers
who had died.
We wanted that feeling
to be carried worldwide

THIRTEEN DEAD
NOTHING SAID

We got our wish
But they got theirs
Next morning as
BLACK RAMPAGE
Was slashed all over
the breakfast table.

We got our wish
An inquest

But they got theirs
A verdict . . . left open.

We will march all our lives
And we will be sore
Until the pain goes away.
We will march some more.

# Yuh Hear Bout?

*Valerie Bloom*

Yuh hear bout di people dem arres
Fi bun dung di Asian people dem house?
Yuh hear bout di policeman dem lock up
Fi beat up di black bwoy widout a cause?
Yuh hear bout di M.P. dem sack because im
    refuse fi help
im coloured constituents in a dem fight
    'gainst deportation?
Yuh noh hear bout dem?
Me neida.

# Listen Mr Oxford Don

*John Agard*

Me not no Oxford don
me a simple immigrant
from Clapham Common
I didn't graduate
I immigrate

But listen Mr Oxford don
I'm a man on de run
and a man on de run
is a dangerous one

I ent have no gun
I ent have no knife
but mugging de Queen's English
is the story of my life

I don't need no axe
to split/up yu syntax
I don't need no hammer
to mash/up yu grammar

I warning you Mr Oxford don
I'm a wanted man
and a wanted man
is a dangerous one

Dem accuse me of assault
on de Oxford dictionary/
imagine a concise peaceful man like me/
dem want me serve time
for inciting rhyme to riot
but I tekking it quiet
down here in Clapham Common

I'm not a violent man Mr Oxford don
I only armed wit mih human breath
but human breath
is a dangerous weapon

So mek dem send one big word after me
I ent serving no jail sentence
I slashing suffix in self-defence
I bashing future wit present tense
and if necessary

I making de Queen's English accessory/to my offence

# Nature's Politics

*Benjamin Zephaniah*

Love and peace
and nuclear-free,
and life and plants
and liberty,
and food and shelter
answer me,
who made it political,
the right to see
the right to view,
the way dis pen now talks to you,
a place where children free to go
now answer me or don't you know,
no need to dream or think too hard
just take a look round your backyard,
for life is nature's miracle –
who made it political???

# Girls Can We Educate We Dads?

*James Berry*

Listn the male chauvinist in mi dad –
a girl walkin night street mus be bad.
He dohn sey, the world's a free place
for a girl to keep her unmolested space.
Instead he sey – a girl is a girl.

He sey a girl walkin swingin hips about
call boys to look and shout.
He dohn sey, if a girl have style
she wahn to sey, look
I okay from top to foot.
Instead he sey – a girl is a girl.

Listn the male chauvinist in mi dad –
a girl too laughy-laughy look too glad-glad
jus like a girl too looky-looky roun
will get a pretty satan at her side.
He dohn sey – a girl full of go
dohn wahn stifle talent comin on show.
Instead he sey – a girl is a girl.

# Measure for Measure

*Sipho Sepamla*

go measure the distance from cape town to pretoria
and tell me the prescribed area i can work in

count the number of days in a year
and say how many of them i can be contracted around

calculate the size of house you think good for me
and ensure the shape suits tribal tastes

measure the amount of light into the window
known to guarantee my traditional ways

count me enough wages to make certain that i
grovel in the mud for more food

teach me just so much of the world that i
can fit into certain types of labour

show me only those kinds of love
which will make me aware of my place at all times

and when all that is done
let me tell you this
you'll never know how far i stand from you

# The Ballot and the Bullet

*Chris Van Wyk*

The ballot.
This means voting.
There's this big box.
It has a slot.
Ja, like a money box.
You're given options.
Do you want a cruel government
or a kind one?
A lazy one
or one that works?
You have to make an X
on a square sheet of paper
to decide who is to be
the custodian of the people.
But first you have to identify yourself.
This is easy.
All you need is an I.D.
This looks like a passbook;
It has your photo and signature.
Only difference is
you can leave it at home
and not get caught.
That's a ballot.
Now a bullet.
Ag now, surely you know
what a bullet is.

# On Judgement Day

*Sipho Sepamla*

black people are born singers
black people are born runners
black people are peace-loving
these myths make of us naivete

we have been sipped with bubbles of champagne
we have known choking dust
and have writhed with the pain of humiliation

singers
runners
peace-loving

nobody really sees the storm raging within us
nobody cares to know that we've reached our own bottom
laughing has become agonizing

singers
runners
peace-loving
my foot

I fear we will all sing at night-vigils
and as I see things we will all run for cover
what I don't know is which peace will still be lovable

# Preacher, Don't Send Me

## *Maya Angelou*

Preacher, don't send me
When I die
to some big ghetto
in the sky
where rats eat cats
of the leopard type
and Sunday brunch
is grits and tripe.

I've known those rats
I've seen them kill
and grits I've had
would make a hill,
or maybe a mountain,
so what I need
from you on Sunday
is a different creed.

Preacher, please don't
promise me
streets of gold
and milk for free.
I stopped all milk
at four years old
and once I'm dead
I won't need gold.

I'd call a place
pure paradise
where families are loyal
and strangers are nice,
where the music is jazz
and the season is fall.
Promise me that
or nothing at all.

# First, They Said

*Alice Walker*

First, they said we were savages.
But we knew how well we had treated them
and knew we were not savages.

Then, they said we were immoral.
But we knew minimal clothing
did not equal immoral.

Next, they said our race was inferior.
But we knew our mothers
and we knew that our race
was not inferior.

After that, they said we were
a backward people.
But we knew our fathers
and knew we were not backward.

So, then they said we were
obstructing Progress.
But we knew the rhythm of our days
and knew that we were not obstructing Progress.

Eventually, they said the truth is that you eat
too much and your villages take up too much
of the land. But we knew we and our children
were starving and our villages were burned
to the ground. So we knew we were not eating
too much or taking up too much of the land.

Finally, they had to agree with us.

They said: You are right. It is not your savagery
or your immorality or your racial inferiority or
your people's backwardness or your obstructing of
Progress or your appetite or your infestation of the land
that is at fault. No. What is at fault
is your existence itself.

Here is money, they said. Raise an army
among your people, and exterminate
yourselves.

In our inferior backwardness
we took the money. Raised an army
among our people.
And now, the people protected, we wait
for the next insulting words
coming out of that mouth.

**Workers'**

**VOICES**

Most people have to work to make a living. Some cannot get work. Some can, but find it very unsatisfactory. In nineteenth-century Britain, it was the conditions in which people lived and worked, and the low pay, that was the source of protest. That feeling of being exploited – or working for inadequate reward – is a common theme in these poems.

Some of the writers complain about the idea of work itself and how it dominates their lives; how it squats like a toad and undermines worthwhile ambitions. Others are concerned that they work at making things they will never be able to afford for themselves, that what they produce has no benefit for them. Whether it is Britain in the nineteenth century, America in the 1930s, Eastern Europe, or South America, the themes remain the same.

Some of the poems protest at the attitude of employers and the way they treat those they employ. And schoolwork, also, comes under fire because it is capable of being boring and can ignore what young people really want to learn.

This section involves a very broad definition of worker, but it embraces all those who feel that their efforts, and those of others like them, are not fairly rewarded by the particular system in which they labour.

# London

*William Blake*

I wander through each chartered street,
Near where the chartered Thames does flow,
And mark in every face I meet
Marks of weakness, marks of woe.

In every cry of every man,
In every infant's cry of fear,
In every voice, in every ban,
The mind-forged manacles I hear.

How the chimney-sweeper's cry
Every blackening church appals;
And the hapless soldier's sigh
Runs in blood down palace walls.

But most through midnight streets I hear
How the youthful harlot's curse
Blasts the new-born infant's tear,
And blights with plagues the marriage hearse.

*from:*

# Child Labour

*Elizabeth Barrett Browning*

'For oh,' say the children, 'we are weary
And we cannot run or leap;
If we care for any meadows, it were merely
To drop down in them and sleep.
Our knees tremble sorely in the stooping,
We fall upon our faces, trying to go;
And underneath our heavy eyelids drooping
The reddest flower would look as pale as snow.
For, all day, we drag our burden tiring
Through the coal-dark, underground;
Or, all day, we drive the wheels of iron
In the factories, round and round.

For all day the wheels are droning, turning;
Their wind comes in our faces,
Till our hearts turn, our heads with pulses burning,
And the walls turn in their places:
Turns the long light that drops adown the wall,
Turn the black flies that crawl along the ceiling:
All are turning, all the day, and we with all.
And all day, the iron wheels are droning,
And sometimes we could pray,
"O ye wheels" (breaking out in mad moaning)
"Stop! Be silent for today!" '

LETTING CHILDREN
DOWN **A** COAL MINE
From a Plate in the *Westminster
Review*

# Questions From A Worker Who Reads

*Bertolt Brecht*

Who built Thebes of the seven gates?
In the books you will find the names of kings.
Did the kings haul up the lumps of rock?
And Babylon, many times demolished
Who raised it up so many times? In what houses
Of gold-glittering Lima did the builders live?
Where, the evening that the Wall of China was
finished
Did the masons go? Great Rome
Is full of triumphal arches. Who erected them?
Over whom
Did the Caesars triumph? Had Byzantium,
much praised in song
Only places for its inhabitants? Even in fabled
Atlantis
The night the ocean engulfed it
The drowning still bawled for their slaves.

The young Alexandra conquered India.
Was he alone?
Caesar beat the Gauls.
Did he not have even a cook with him?
Philip of Spain wept when his armada
Went down. Was he the only one to weep?
Frederick the Second won the Seven Years' War.
Who else won it?

Every page a victory.
Who cooked the feast for the victors?
Every ten years a great man.
Who paid the bill?

So many reports.
So many questions.

# Toads

*Philip Larkin*

Why should I let the toad *work*
　　Squat on my life?
Can't I use my wit as a pitchfork
　　And drive the brute off?

Six days of the week it soils
　　With its sickening poison –
Just for paying a few bills!
　　That's out of proportion.

Lots of folk live on their wits:
　　Lecturers, lispers,
Losels, loblolly-men, louts –
　　They don't end as paupers;

Lots of folk live up lanes
　　With fires in a bucket,
Eat windfalls and tinned sardines –
　　They seem to like it.

Their nippers have got bare feet,
　　Their unspeakable wives
Are skinny as whippets – and yet
　　No one actually *starves*.

Ah, were I courageous enough
　　To shout *Stuff your pension*!
But I know, all too well, that's the stuff
　　That dreams are made on:

For something sufficiently toad-like
　　Squats in me, too;
Its hunkers are heavy as hard luck,
　　And cold as snow,

And will never allow me to blarney
   My way to getting
The fame and the girl and the money
   All at one sitting.

I don't say, one bodies the other
   One's spiritual truth;
But I do say it's hard to lose either,
   When you have both.

# Untitled

*Jeltje*

I can't face work.
I'll turn my back on it.
I turn my back on it.
I've turned my back on it.

# Next Summer

*T. A. Stancliffe*

He asked for bread,
    They promised instead,
A job – next summer.

Then congress met,
    They voted – you bet,
A job – next summer.

Big business said,
    With nodding head,
A job – next summer.

If this will check,
    I'll have – by heck,
A dozen jobs – next summer.

# Casualty

*Miroslav Holub*

They bring us crushed fingers,
mend it, doctor.
They bring burnt-out eyes,
hounded owls of hearts,
they bring a hundred white bodies,
a hundred red bodies,
and a hundred black bodies,
mend it, doctor,
on the dishes of ambulances they bring
the madness of blood,
the scream of flesh,
the silence of charring,
mend it, doctor.
And while we are suturing
inch after inch,
night after night,
nerve to nerve,
muscle to muscle,
eyes to sight,
they bring in
even longer daggers,
even more thunderous bombs,
even more glorious victories,

idiots.

# Three Poems for Women

*Susan Griffin*

This is a poem for women doing dishes.
This is a poem for women doing dishes.
It must be repeated.
It must be repeated,
again and again,
again and again,
because the woman doing dishes
because the woman doing dishes
has trouble hearing
has trouble hearing.

And this is another poem for a woman
cleaning the floor
who cannot hear at all.
Let us have a moment of silence
for the woman who cleans the floor.

And here is one more poem
for the woman at home
with children.
You never see her at night.
Stare at an empty space and imagine her there,
the woman with children
because she cannot be here to speak
for herself,
and listen
to what you think
she might say.

**Your hands won't suffer if you wash up this way**

Just a little Quix takes all the drudgery out of washing-up, yet keeps your hands soft and smooth. It kills grease at once and makes the job so much easier and quicker. No smears on china and glass, no greasy ring round the bowl.

Home-cleaning **TIPS!**

So many jobs around the house are quicker and easier with Quix. Windows, tiles, baths, paintwork — all shine without smears after a quick rub-over with Quix. And carpets, upholstery, come up like new — grease and dirt just vanish! See for yourself.

# Quix

**I'3d Per Bottle**

*Takes the "oh dear" out of washing-up*

QX 45-1400                    CROSFIELDS (C W G) LIMITED, WARRINGTON

# Florida Road Workers

*Langston Hughes*

I'm makin' a road
For the cars
To fly by on.
Makin' a road
Through the palmetto* thicket

For a light and civilization
To travel on.

Makin' a road
For the rich old white men
To sweep over in their big cars
And leave me standin' here.

Sure,
A road helps all of us!
White folks ride –
And I get to see 'em ride.
I ain't never seen nobody
Ride so fine before.
Hey buddy!
Look at me.
I'm making a road!

(* palm tree)

# I Hate the Company Bosses

*Sarah Ogan Gunning*

I hate the company bosses,
I'll tell you the reason why.
They cause me so much suffering
And my dearest friends to die.

Oh yes, I guess you wonder
What they have done to me.
I'm going to tell you, mister,
My husband had T.B.

Brought on by hard work and low wages
And not enough to eat,
Going naked and hungry,
No shoes on his feet.

I guess you'll say he's lazy
And did not want to work.
But I must say you're crazy,
For work he did not shirk.

My husband was a coal miner,
He worked and risked his life
To try to support three children,
Himself, his mother, and wife.

I had a blue-eyed baby,
The darling of my heart.
But from my little darling
Her mother had to part.

Those mighty company bosses,
They dress in jewels and silk.
But my darling blue-eyed baby,
She starved to death for milk.

I had a darling mother
For her I often cry.
But with them rotten conditions
My mother had to die.

Well, what killed your mother?
Oh tell us, if you please.
Excuse me, it was pellagra,
That starvation disease.

They call this the land of plenty,
To them I guess it's true
But that's to the company bosses
Not workers like me and you.

Well, what can I do about it,
To these men of power and might?
I tell you, company bosses,
I'm going to fight, fight, fight.

What can we do about it,
To right this dreadful wrong?
We're all going to join the union,
For the union makes us strong.

# Spic Take the Broom

*Pedro Pietri*

Spic take the broom
and sweep the place
till you make it look
cleaner than heaven
Spic take the mop
and baptize the floor
with soap and water
Spic the garbage can
looks like your salary
make it look like
my salary immediately
Spic I feel hungry
run faster than the speed
of light and get me
a tailored made sandwich
Spic skip your lunch today
for coming late yesterday
Spic I is feeling bored
amuse me with your
broken English humour
Spic the floor is sinning
again do your thing
with the salvation broom
Spic the windows are blind
restore their vision
Spic you have five minutes
to make ten deliveries
Spic stick your tongue out
I want to mail a letter
Spic say goodnight
to your employer he is
exhausted from looking
as you work so hard.

# Me Aunty Connie

*Terry Lee*

They make cakes at Carson's.
Enormously sticky ones
With dollops of cream on top,
Jam tarts and doughnuts
Fancy eclairs,
All made at Carson's.
Me Aunty worked at Carson's,
On the cream button.
She put the dollop on the cake
As it passed along the conveyor belt.
She'd been there fifteen years
Then she was promoted
To Senior Cream Dolloper.
It carried responsibility,
And extra buttons.
She had to ensure
No cakes were eaten.
It was instant dismissal at Carson's
To eat a cake.

Laughing and talking
Was also forbidden.
If she'd stayed another fifteen years,
She'd have been promoted again
To the packing machine
What puts the cakes in boxes,
To take them to the shops.
But she didn't stay.
She was offered a higher paid job.
And on her last day,
She dolloped the wrong cakes.
And the Chelsea buns
Went through with cream on them,
While the gateaus went without.
And the foreman blew his whistle
And stopped production.

The emergency light went on
And the manager came down.
Everyone was laughing and talking.
When he asked her why she did it,
She said she wanted to.
Course she got dismissal instantly.
But she didn't care.
On the way out,
She picked up a cake
And ate it in front of him.
Everyone at Carson's
Knows me Aunty Connie.

# Common Sense

### Alan Brownjohn

An agricultural labourer, who has
A wife and four children, receives 20s a week
¾ buys food, and the members of the family
Have three meals a day.
How much is that per person per meal?
  – From Pitman's Common Sense Arithmetic, 1917

A gardener, paid 24s a week, is
Fined ⅓ if he comes to work late.
At the end of 26 weeks, he receives
£30.5.3. How
Often was he late?
  – From Pitman's Common Sense Arithmetic, 1917

A milk dealer buys milk at 3d a quart. He
Dilutes it with 3% water and sells
124 gallons of the mixture at
4d per quart. How much of his profit is made by
Adulterating the milk?
  – From Pitman's Common Sense Arithmetic, 1917

The table printed below gives the number
Of paupers in the United Kingdom, and
The total cost of poor relief.
Find the average number
Of paupers per ten thousand people.
  – From Pitman's Common Sense Arithmetic, 1917

An army had to march to the relief of
A besieged town, 500 miles away, which
Had telegraphed that it could hold out for 18 days.
The army made forced marches at the rate of 18
Miles a day. Would it be there in time?
  – From Pitman's Common Sense Arithmetic, 1917

Out of an army of 28,000 men,
15% were
Killed, 25% were
Wounded. Calculate
how many men there were left to fight.

*– From Pitman's Common Sense Arithmetic, 1917*

These sums are offered to
That host of young people in our Elementary Schools,
    who
Are so ardently desirous of setting
Foot upon the first rung of the
Educational ladder. . . .

*– From Pitman's Common Sense Arithmetic, 1917*

# Schoolroom on a Wet Afternoon

*Vernon Scannell*

The unrelated paragraphs of morning
Are forgotten now: the severed heads of kings
Rot by the misty Thames: the rose of York
And Lancaster are pressed between the leaves
Of history; negroes sleep in Africa.
The complexities of simple interest lurk
In inkwells and the brittle sticks of chalk:
Afternoon is come and English Grammar.

Rain falls as though the sky has been bereaved,
Stutters its inarticulate grief on glass
Of every lachrymose pane. The children read
Their books or make pretence of concentration,
Each bowed head seems bent in supplication
Or resignation to the fate that waits
In the unmapped forests of the future.
Is it their doomed innocence noon weeps for?

In each diminutive breast a human heart
Pumps out the necessary blood: desires,
Pains and ecstasies surfride each singing wave
Which breaks in darkness on the mental shores.
Each child is disciplined; absorbed and still
At his small desk. Yet lift the lid and see,
Amidst frayed books and pencils, other shapes:
Vicious rope, glaring blade, the gun cocked to kill.

# Prisoners' VOICES

All the prisoners represented here were political prisoners. They were imprisoned for their beliefs, and opposition to a political system or regime, not for criminal acts. Most, if not all, will have faced mental and physical torture. Many of the poems were smuggled out of prison and the authors, probably by choice, remain anonymous.

The details of human rights abuses are reported by Amnesty International and it is through them that many of these poems have come to light. We know of the brutal torture and killings of prisoners in Chile after the 1973 military coup. Ariel Dorfman has written poems dedicated to the 'disappeared' in Chile. Conditions were similar in Uruguay, where poems were smuggled out of prison on cigarette papers.

Nelson Mandela is the most famous of South Africa's political prisoners, but there are many others, including Dennis Brutus and Jeremy Cronin. The poems here were written in the 1960s and 1970s.

Elsewhere, the anonymous poet of 'The Doves' was imprisoned and then tortured by the Iranian secret police during the rule of the Shah for writing an 'unpopular' book. Irina Ratushinskaya was sentenced to seven years' hard labour in the USSR in 1983 for writing poetry. Her poems were smuggled out of prison on tiny sheets of paper.

The first poem in this section was written during a Suffragette hunger strike in 1912.

# Holloway Prison, 1912

*Anonymous*

There was a small woman called G,
Who smashed two big windows at B –
They sent her to jail, her fate to bewail,
For Votes must be kept, must be kept for the male.

They asked that small woman called G,
Why she smashed those big windows at B –
She made a long speech, then made her defence.

But it wasn't no use, their heads were so dense;
They just hummed the refrain, altho' it is stale –
Votes must be kept, must be kept for the male.

They sent her to H for six months and a day,
In the coach Black Maria she went sadly away;
But she sang in this strain, as it jolted and rumbled,
We will have the Vote, we will not be humbled.
We must have the Vote by hill and by dale,
Votes shall not alone be kept for the male.

# From a Chilean Prison, 1973

*Anonymous*

Two by two
four unjust metres
a gift from the four generals.
My solitude knows this world:
Two by two
four square metres in this gaol
is the justice of the generals.
From today on my cell is incommunicado,
prisoner without communication:
a person facing the world
not to be communicated with.

# Speaking with the Children

*Anonymous*

It so happens that I won't be home tomorrow either
and I'll continue beneath the night
that eclipses and erodes
the profiles of the world I know.

If it comes to pass
that I get lost during the night
and don't find the road back home,
I want you to know the reason for my absence.

I have learned and I have taught that a person is free,
and now I awake to the rattling of irons and bolts;
the flames have fed themselves with my books.

I did not stain my spirit with hatred,
but I have seen the anguish
of the epileptic terror
of naked men being electrocuted.

I returned to the road the peasants used,
speaking of a life without miseries.
I explained that work brings dignity
and that there is no bread at all
without a sheaf of wheat made noble
by the planting of a seed into the earth
by simple hand.

For this, among other things,
it so happens,
that I won't be home tomorrow either
but continue beneath the night.

# Last Will and Testament

*Ariel Dorfman*

When they tell you
I'm not a prisoner
don't believe them.
They'll have to admit it
some day.
When they tell you
they released me
don't believe them.
They'll have to admit
it's a lie
some day.
When they tell you
I betrayed the party
don't believe them.
They'll have to admit
I was loyal
some day.

Don't believe them,
don't believe
anything they tell you
anything they swear to
anything they show you,
don't believe them.

And finally when
that day comes
when they ask you
to identify the body
and you see me
and a voice says
we killed him
the poor bastard died
he's dead,
when they tell you
that I am
completely absolutely definitely
dead
don't believe them,
don't believe them,
don't believe them.

# Two Poems from La Libertad

*Anonymous*

TO HAVE a quick word with the bee
in its buzzing flight
to ask the ant to hurry
with the bread
for his lady wife
to contemplate the spider
admire the beauty
of its amazing feat
and beg it
to climb more slowly up its web
all these are ways
of resisting.


A FELLOW inmate said
if we put aside
orders
regulations
if we overlook
uniforms
bars
if we don't count
officers
and their stool-pigeons
a fellow inmate said
and I believe him
here
in this great prison
we are not prisoners.

*La Libertad prison for male political prisoners*

# Cold

*Dennis Brutus*

the clammy cement
sucks our naked feet

a rheumy yellow bulb
lights a damp grey wall

the stubbled grass
wet with three o'clock dew
is black with glittery edges;

we sit on the concrete,
stuff with our fingers
the sugarless pap
into our mouths

then labour erect;

form lines;

steel ourselves into fortitude
or accept an image of ourselves
numb with resigned acceptance;
the grizzled senior warder comments:

'Things like these
I have no time for;

they are worse than rats;
you can only shoot them.'

Overhead
the large frosty glitter of the stars
the Southern Cross flowering low;

the chains on our ankles
and wrists
that pair us together
jangle

glitter.

We begin to move
        awkwardly.

# Letter to Martha

*Dennis Brutus*

I remember rising one night
after midnight
and moving
through an impulse of loneliness
to try and find the stars.

And through the haze
the battens of fluorescents made
I saw pinpricks of white
I thought were stars.

Greatly daring
I thrust my arm through the bars
and easing the switch in the corridor
plunged my cell in darkness

I scampered to the window
and saw the splashes of light
where the stars flowered.

But through my delight
thudded the anxious boots
and a warning barked
from the machine-gun post
on the catwalk.

And it is the brusque inquiry
and threat
that I remember of that night
rather than the stars.

# Inside

*Jeremy Cronin*

Overhead is mesh,
To one side the morgue,
To one side the gallows wing, this
Is our yard

Into which a raggedy
By happenstance
Butterfly has flown,

Fluttering
Halfway to panic
Halfway to give a damn

Springtime has come.
The years flow into each other.
The struggle goes on.

# A Person is a Person Because of Other People

*Jeremy Cronin*

By holding my mirror out of the window I see
Clear to the end of the passage.
There's a person down there.
A prisoner polishing a doorhandle.
In the mirror I see him see
My face in the mirror,
I see the fingertips of his free hand
Bunch together, as if to make
An object the size of a badge
Which travels up to his forehead
The place of an imaginary cap.
          (This means: *A warder*).
Two fingers are extended in a vee
And wiggle like two antennae.
          (He's being watched.)
A finger of his free hand makes a watch-hand's arc
On the wrist of his polishing arm without
Disrupting the slow-slow rhythm of his work.
          (*Later*. Maybe, later we can speak.)
*Hey! Wat maak jy daar?*
          – a voice from around the corner.
*No. Just polishing baas.*
He turns his back to me, now watch
His free hand, the talkative one,
Slips quietly behind
          – *Strength brother*, it says,
In my mirror,
          A black fist.

# The Doves

*Anonymous*

Outside doves perch everywhere.
It is clear from
their cooings of love and delight;
It is clear from
the whirr of their wings;
wings which seem to fan me in my prisoner's sleep.
It is clear that outside
doves perch everywhere.

The night is like day on the other side of the bars;
on this side the day is like night.

# Not the Execution

*Halfdan Rasmussen*

Not the execution scares me
not the hate and the torture
not the death by rifles
not the shadow on the wall
not the nights of pain
when the last star falls
but the merciless world's
blind indifference.

# It's Not That I'm Scared

*Irina Ratushinskaya*

It's not that I'm scared,
Just a little uneasy.
It hurts that I might not bear a son,
As the heart is giving out, and the hands grow weaker –
I try to hold on,
But they just grow weaker, damn them!
I could have written children's books,
And I liked horses,
And also I liked to perch on a favourite cliff,
And jumping into the sea I could pace myself well;
And when I thought I could not get back
I'd still somehow swim to shore.
And I flew in my dreams and shuddered
When I thought my time would come soon.
But the voice had spoken: 'If not I, then who?'
It had spoken so long ago –
I had no choice in the matter.
For they are shameful the endless debates over tea,
For they have perished – the brightest and the best!
Father Alexander, pray for those on the sea –
And for the land
They have left behind.

# Pencil Letter

*Irina Ratushinskaya*

I know it won't be received
Or sent. The page will be
In shreds as soon as I have scribbled it.
Later. Sometime. You've grown used to it,
Reading between the lines that never reached you,
Understanding everything. On the tiny sheet,
Not making haste, I find room for the night.
What's the hurry, when the hour that's passed
Is all part of the same time, the same unknown term.
The word stirs under my hand
Like a starling, a rustle, a movement of eyelashes.
Everything's fine. But don't come into my dream yet.
In a little while I will tie my sadness into a knot,
Throw my head back and on my lips there'll be a seal,
A smile, my prince, although from afar.
Can you feel the warmth of my hand
Passing through your hair, over your hollow cheek.
December winds have blown on your face . . .
How thin you are . . . Stay in my dream.
Open the window. The pillow is hot.
Footsteps at the door, and a bell tolling in the tower:
Two, three . . . Remember, you and I never said
Goodbye. It doesn't matter.
Four o'clock . . . That's it. How heavily it tolls.

A photograph smuggled out of the Soviet labour camp,
Mordovia, Barashevo Settlement

# Touch

*Hugh Lewin*

When I get out
I'm going to ask someone
   to touch me
   very gently please
   and slowly,
   touch me
   I want
   to learn again
   how life feels.

I've not been touched
for seven years
   for seven years
   I've been untouched
   out of touch
   and I've learnt
   to know now
   the meaning of
   untouchable.

Untouched - not quite
I can count the things
that have touched me

One: fists
At the beginning
   fierce mad fists
   beating beating
   till I remember
   screaming
   Don't touch me
   please don't touch me.

Two: paws
The first four years of paws
   every day
   patting paws, searching
   – arms up, shoes off
   legs apart –
   prodding paws, systematic
   heavy, indifferent
   probing away
   all privacy.

I don't want fists and paws
I want
   to want to be touched
   again
   and to touch,
   I want to feel alive
   again
   I want to say
   when I get out
Here I am
please touch me.

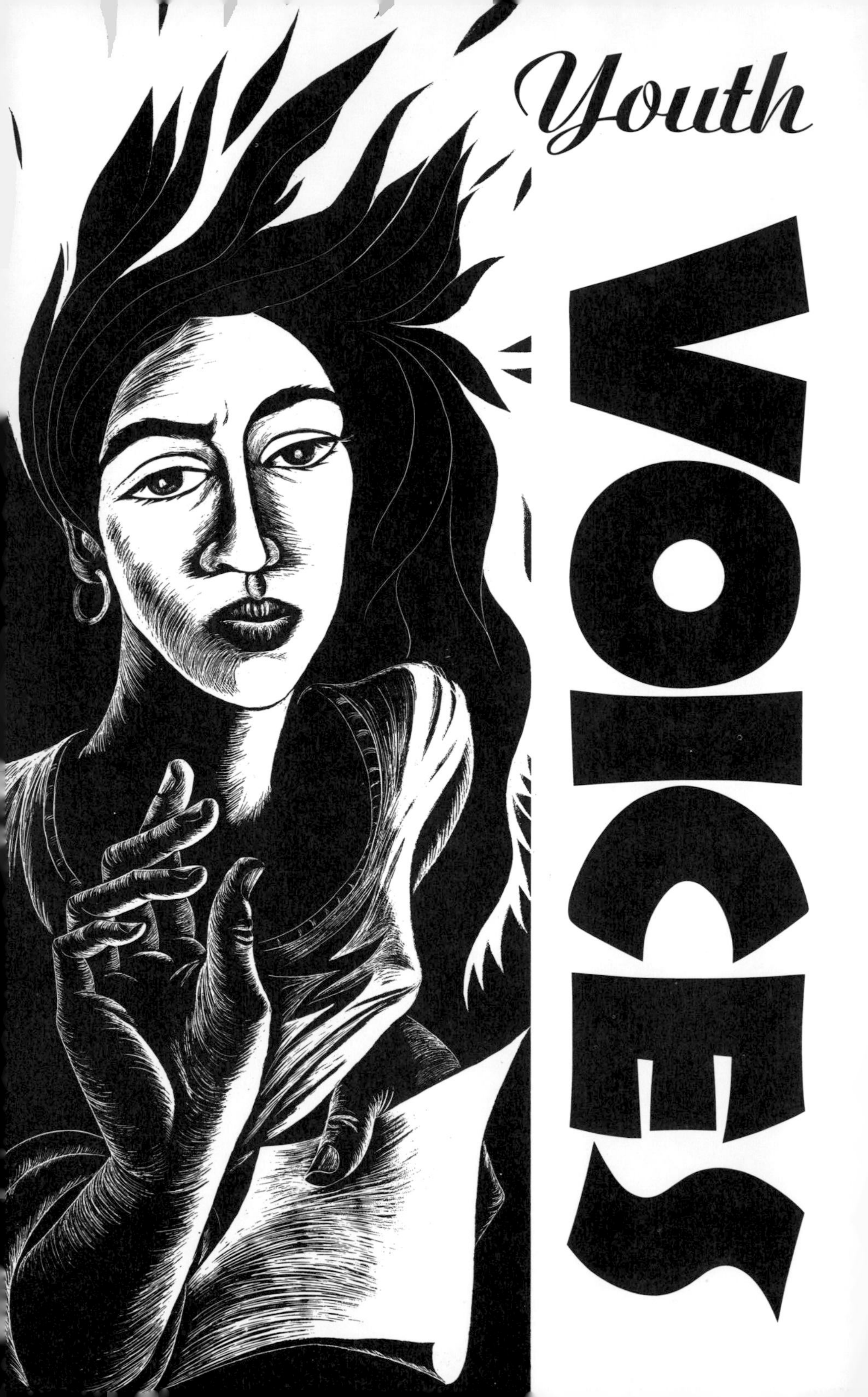
Youth
VOICES

' "Youth is a permanent excuse for giving pain." Discuss.'
was the title of an essay question set for an English exam
some years ago. The statement assumes that young people
are bound to have different ideas, but it's just a part of
growing up. And anyway, these ideas are pretty worthless.

The poems here suggest otherwise; that young people are
genuinely concerned about the world they inhabit and pos-
sess the skill to articulate those concerns in poetic form.
War, racism, sexism, school, the environment, the pres-
sures of life – all the concerns of adults also. The voice of
youth is a very mature voice.

All the poems here were written in the period 1989–91 by
school students.

# Behind Closed Doors

*Matthew Davies*

The door was different.
It opened, closed,
and frightened the life out of us.

Its deep blue paintwork
reminded me of the sea;
adventurers and pirates

might conquer this door,
sail through it
and discover some forgotten land
or treasure.

And as far as I was concerned

they could have it

because behind that door
was a woman

a woman more tyrannical than Mrs Thatcher
a woman with more scruples than Mary Whitehouse
a woman with more pairs of shoes
than Imelda Marcos;

it was the headmistress
and I was in for it.

# Thro' the Keyhole

*Judith Peel*

My cracked and pitted lips begged for mercy,
A dribble of blood trickled down my dusty chin,
And splashed on the hard, unyielding floor,
My throat had constricted,
'Til my breath barely escaped me.

My cell offered little haven from the elements,
Where in hot days my sweat
Had bathed the grey stone floor,
And in the nights my shivering body,
Huddled against the moss-speckled walls,
Yielded naught but cries.

But thro' the keyhole . . .

White-washed buildings were sun-freckled and clean,
Shone like bright pennies,
And the air was laced with songs of God.
'God!' I spat the word,
God that had forsaken me.

But if I could leave the village,
And walk in the dew-sodden grass,
And see the green sun-dappled mist,
Wade bare-foot in icy springs,
Splash the tiny water-droplets,
Up to the sun,
To shine as perfect diamonds.

My cell is grey,
Grey with age
My age,
My frustration rings out,
My hands strike metal,
Metal and flesh coverse,
Blood drips, no-one to care.

But thro' the keyhole . . .

Children play,
But a foot step away.

# Not In India

*Sadi Husain*

'I want a proper bag,' I cried.
'But this is a proper bag.
In India we always took these to school.'
'We're not in India!'
'Go on, go to school, Craig is here,' ordered Mum.
Craig, his clean pink face beaming a smile,
had his bag across his back.
My satchel laboured at my hip,
constantly trying to get away.

We arrive in school, late for prayers again. Good.
Spelling test. Easy. Full marks.
'This boy came to Britain when he was six.
He couldn't speak English.
Now he's a better speller than all of you.'
Maths, just long division and fractions.
'Indians are always good at Maths,' Mum used to say.
Geography. Maps. Places I haven't seen.
'Sadi came to Wales two years ago and now he knows
all the countries in the world.'

Leaving school for another day.
A boy runs shouting 'Chocolate!'
Craig defends me, 'Then you're a Milky Bar!'
'But I'm not chocolate, I'm just like you!' I think.
'Home already?
In India we didn't come home 'til five,' said Mum.

'But we're not in India, are we?' I cried,
running upstairs and locking the door behind me.

# Pet Hates

*Amy Barnard*

The poor dog's cigarette craving
Has been caused by the scientist's raving
To find a new cure for the rich and for poor.
Lucky dog! Think of all the coupons he's saving.

The great whale should not give up hope,
Its back speared with harpoon and rope.
Its soul will stay clean, sparkle and sheen
When it's stuck in a big bar of soap.

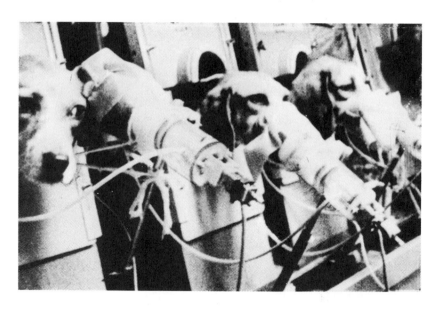

# Waiter! There's an Elephant in My Soup

*David McWilliams*

A shaking head, a snap of fingers,
A Waiter at his side.
His world in ruins, an elephant,
In the soup of mankind.

His great creations: humans,
To vultures; circling over carrion prey.
Too idle to fight, just steal.
In an endless wait, to see the light of day.

Mansions and blankets,
Famines and banquets.
Freedom and borders,
Wartime deaths and orders.
Paupers and men without cares,
Pennies in a jar, and stockmarket shares.
From the colour of your shoes and skin,
To the colour of your cares.
From the colour in your pocket,
To the prices of your shares.

A world for us was made.
To prosper from and enjoy it.
Now man is in charge,
He's going to destroy it.

# Animals Never Forget

*Alexandra Hopkins*

The penguins lie on the rocks
and stare out to sea.

The gulls sit on the cliffs
and stare up at the sky.

The sheep on land
stand
and stare at their feet.

The penguins remember
the big steel monsters, especially
the queer one that went under water
but never rose for air.
They remember the bright yellows,
oranges and reds that illuminated the sky
and the cries
and the screams of
the two-legged, land-living animals
who didn't swim.

The gulls remember
the strange, shiny birds
that dived and climbed
and spat fire
and crashed and exploded.
They remember the distorted faces on
the two-legged, land-living animals
who didn't get the chance to show
they couldn't fly.

The sheep remember
the big metal boxes
which made the strange tracks,
and the four-wheeled vehicles
and the flocks of humans
bewildered, bemused and waiting
for the intimidating whistle
that would make them
into none-legged, dead, land animals.

Now all is tranquil on the islands.
But for how long?
Until the 'question of sovereignty'
is raised once more.

# Women Are...

*Julia Stubbs*

Women are . . .
or are they?
Is it more a case of what men say,
what their little minds expect
of the women they protect?
'A woman should be faithful,
considerate and kind,
do housework and bear children,
leave all careers behind.
A woman needs security,
a life of domesticity,
romance and sensitivity'
and her slavery papers signed!
Should men see their partners
in this chauvinistic way?
An attitude which highlights
a considerate array
of what a woman
wants and needs or
what she should be like –
an adolescent portrait
of a robot on a bike.
Things done automatically,
options are forbidden,
this metaphoric bicycle
is not here to be ridden.

Peter
Robinson

Peter
Robinson
pantaloon £7.95
top £7.95

separates ground floor

# The Price of War

*Alex Cole*

If you should happen to chance upon
My grave, and shed a tear,
The epitaph on it should read,
'A naive man died here.'

'Come along, help Britain win!'
The bright war posters cry.
'You'll be a hero overnight,'
That dirty, dreadful lie.

The prospect seemed a good one,
The thought struck my empty head.
It struck again in a mud-filled trench,
And then it struck me dead.

If being a hero tempts you,
Don't let it take hold.
War is going to cost you dear;
It's fatal, being bold.

# Do You Care?

*Rachel Slade*

Do you think of me
When you're out for the night
Exercising your human rights?
Do you think of me
When you go to work
Making eyes at the boss and flirt?

Do you think of me
And the life I've had?
Or are the memories too painful and too bad?
Or don't you believe that in the womb
A human life and soul's entombed?
That at twenty-four weeks
A switch in heaven's turned on
And that is when human life is begun.
I suppose you chose to ignore
The baby that was born before
The fact that then it had arms and feet
And a tiny little heart that beat.

What about my rights, mother dear?
My rights to laugh, to see, to hear,
To have freedom of speech,
To express myself,
To experience love, happiness and health.

I never have and never will
Hold a hand, smile at you.

Will you think of me
When you hold your first born child?
Will you think of me
When you see it smile?
Will you ever think of me, mother dear?

# Hate

*Sally-Anne Clark*

The cloud in a clear sky
Is distorted in the brain
Till all reason is gone.

The cloud is grey,
Ominous, angry,
Tells of a storm to come.

The cloud is seen
And people put up umbrellas
So as not to get wet.

The cloud fills the sky
Thunderous and deadly.
But rainstorms pass. . . .

The cloud bursts.
But no water falls
Only violence and obscenities.

The cloud is gone.
So are the people.

# A Shout in the Silence

*Aisling Hogan*

I live in a frozen forest of burning chains,
And drown in a muddy pool of dependent love.
I shout to be heard, but the silence steals my words
And throws them aside on the rocks of inadequacy.
I run to keep up, but still I fall further behind,
With hungry orphans who grab at my thread-bare rags.
I feast at the tables of rich and mighty men,
While all around me the world is shattered and burned.

I live as a slave to normality –
A suburban housewife in my teens.
I'm the crucial runner in a human race
Until at last I fall and start to tire.
They'll throw my breathing body on the pyre
And then perhaps I'll face the screaming sea
And launch myself into eternity.

# A Feather or a Hand

*Theodora Crow*

The gnarled feather of dark tracing paper skin and bone
A hand compressed by a famined land
It lies in the grip of an affluent white,
This feather-like hand.

Can it wave, this hand, this dark
impoverished hand on its thread-like wrist?
Can it wave or would it snap?
Does it need to be cradled there, in the palm
of the affluent white?

Would it turn to dust and blow away,
if released from the white man's grip?
Indeed is it really a hand at all,
not a skeleton leaf or a rolling twig?

# Reading and Responding to the Poems

## A first read

A poem needs to be read two or three times to get a sense of its meaning and, preferably, it should be read aloud. Reading aloud helps you get a feel of the rhythm and mood of a poem and to develop your own response. If you can work with someone, or in a group, then you can read the poem to each other and compare your versions.

- Did you read the poem at the same pace, or in the same tone of voice?
- Did you have the same sense of who was writing the poem and for whom it was intended?
- Did you agree on the theme of the poem?
- Did you find you were sympathetic to the poem's theme?
- Did you like it?

**Listen to the reading on the audio cassette:**

- What did you think of that?
- How does it compare with your reading?

## Assignment

In a pair, or group, choose three or four poems to read aloud to each other. You could choose:

- poems on the same theme (e.g. male attitudes)
- poems about a country (e.g. South Africa)
- poems with a humorous tone (e.g. 'Men Talk', 'Preacher Don't Send Me', 'Me Aunty Connie', 'Spic Take The Broom')
- poems written in dialect (e.g. 'XWORDS', 'Yuh Hear Bout?', 'Listen Mr Oxford Don')
- poems written before the twentieth century (e.g. 'The Wife's Complaint', 'The Caged Bird','London', 'Child Labour')

Read, compare and discuss the poems and make notes on the discussion. Your notes should include:

- the content of each poem
- similarities and differences in tone and style
- who is speaking the poem? Is it the author, or another voice?

- what it is about them that would interest a reader
- what difficulties a reader might have understanding them

Assemble your poems as if they were in an anthology and use your notes to write an introduction. Select some photographs or pictures to put with the poems and you will have constructed your own poetry anthology.

## Closer reading

There are a number of strategies that can help you get to grips with a poem. Once again, it helps a lot if you work with someone else.

a) **Titles and first lines**
Sometimes it is worth spending a few minutes jotting down ideas that you get from reading the title or the first line of a poem. What for example do you think of with the title 'Toads' or with the first line 'The unrelated paragraphs of morning'?

b) **Words omitted**
Ask your partner to read a poem in which you deleted a number of key words. Explain what words have been deleted but not their original places in the poem. Ask your partner to select a word for each gap. When your partner has done this, discuss the clues that determined the choice.

c) **Sequencing**
Offer a poem to your partner with the lines in the wrong order. Ask your partner to rewrite the poem in an order that makes the best sense. Then compare with the original version. Try it with the poem 'Holding My Beads'.

You can also experiment with all the verses in the wrong sequence. Try it with 'London'. Ask your partner to unravel the poem.

## Assignment
Work as pairs. Choose a poem and ask each other the following questions:

1 What, in a sentence, is the poem about?
2 Is the poem a story, a monologue, a letter, a call for help, an out-and-out protest, or something else?

3 What is the language of the poem? Standard English, regional dialect, creole? What effect does this language have on you?
4 What is the mood or atmosphere of the poem? Is it tragic, comic, joyful, romantic?
5 Are there any strong images, or pictures, created by the language?
6 Do you think the poem is for reading to a large audience or an individual one? How do you react to hearing the poem? Would others react differently?
7 Do you like the poem? Does it relate to your own views or experience?

Use both sets of answers to construct a written response to the poem.

## Wider reading

### Assignment
Choose a selection of poems from the anthology, linked by theme. Plan and write a response using the following structure:
1 an introduction explaining your choice
2 an explanation of the similarities between poems in terms of content, style, tone, language, rhythm
3 an explanation of the differences
4 a selection of particularly striking words, or lines and images
5 how you imagine the poem being read and being received by different audiences
6 in what way the poems have encouraged you to rethink your view of the world

### Further assignments
Many of the poems here could be 'rewritten' as stories, newspaper articles or even as short plays. The subject matter may inspire you to write your own poetry. Use a poem as a model or a stimulus for your own writing.

# Notes

## Women's Voices

'The Wife's Complaint'

> This is a medieval poem, presumed written by a woman.

'Rondeau Redoublé' means, roughly, going round and round in circles.

> *Zen* – short for Zen Buddhism, a religious belief popular with some youth in the 1960s.
> *Ode* – a long and usually elaborate poem, dedicated to somebody or something.

'Monologue'

> *crèche* – place for supervised care of young children.
> *premenstrual tension* mental or physical symptoms experienced by some women prior to a period.

'I Coming Back'

> '*massa*' – 'master'.
> '*higue*' – in Guyanan folklore, a kind of vampire that sucks the blood *from* babies.

'Two Sketches'

> *Hiroshima* – Japanese city hit by first atomic bomb in 1945.

'Bipeds, Beware'

> *biped* – species with two feet.

## Black Voices

'Colonisation in Reverse'

> The title refers to the emigration of people from the Caribbean to England in the 1950s, in response to advertisements for jobs in Britain in hospitals and public transport because of a labour shortage at the time. Britain originally colonised the Caribbean islands in the seventeenth century.

'Telephone Conversation'

> Black people faced open discrimination when they arrived in Britain. Cards in shop windows advertising rooms might say: 'No Coloureds Need Apply'. This form of discrimination was made illegal in the 1960s.
> *Button A. Button B* – buttons in the old-style telephone kiosk. When pressed, Button A connected you; Button B refunded your money.

'Di Great Insoreckshan'

> *Brixton*, in South London, was one of a number of inner city communities to experience rioting in 1981.
> *Swamp Eight-Wan* – Swamp '81 was the name the police gave to their operations in the Brixton area.
> *Scarman* – Lord Scarman was a judge who carried out an inquiry into the rioting.

'Nothing Said'

> The poem is concerned with the outbreak of a fire during a party at a house in Deptford, London. Thirteen young black people died. The cause of the fire is disputed.

'Listen Mr Oxford Don'

> *Oxford Don* – lecturer at Oxford University.
> *Queen's English* – Standard English.
> *syntax* – word order in a sentence.

'The Ballot and the Bullet'

> *I.D.* – personal identification.

**Workers' Voices**

'London' and 'Child Labour' are nineteenth-century poems.
'Next Summer', 'Florida Road Workers' and 'I Hate the Company Bosses' were written in the USA in the 1930s during the time of 'the depression'.

**Prisoners' Voices**

'Poem from Holloway Prison, 1912'

The Suffragette movement in the early part of the century successfully achieved votes for women in Britain. A number of prisoners went on hunger strike to publicise their cause and were forcibly fed.

'From a Chilean Prison', 'Speaking with the Children', 'Last Will and Testament'

General Pinochet led a military coup in Chile in 1973, overthrowing an elected government. Imprisonment and torture became widespread. Thousands were killed: men, women and children.

'Two poems from La Libertad'

La Libertad – the main prison in Uruguay is called 'Liberty'!
stool-pigeons – inmates who give information to prison officers and therefore cannot be trusted by other prisoners.

# Acknowledgements

Recordings on an accompanying cassette (ISBN 0 582 08548 9, only available to schools) are taken from the BBC School Radio series GCSE English: The Poetry of Protest. The series was produced by Colin Smith and Simon Fuller.

Acknowledgement is due to the following, whose permission is required for multiple reproduction:

POLYGON for 'Men Talk' and 'Man Monologue' by Liz Lochhead taken from New Cliches and True Confessions; 'Rondeau Redouble' by Wendy Cope reprinted by permission of FABER AND FABER LTD taken from Making Cocoa for Kingsley Amis; JANICE GALLOWAY for 'XWords'; 'The Dolphins' taken from Standing Female Nude by Carol Ann Duffy, published by ANVIL PRESS POETRY in 1985; KARNAK HOUSE for 'Holding My Beads' and 'I Coming Back' by Grace Nichols from the collection I is a Long Memory Woman © 1983 and 1990; GILLIAN ALLNUTT for 'Two Sketches'; PLUTO PRESS for 'Bipeds, Beware' by Hazel Archard taken from Poems for Peace; CARCANET PRESS LTD for 'Soviet Invasion of Afghanistan' by Sujata Bhatt taken from Brunizem; OXFORD UNIVERSITY PRESS for 'The Telephone Call' by Fleur Adcock taken from The Incident Book (OUP 1986); CAROLINE SHELDON LITERARY AGENCY for 'Half-caste' and 'Listen Mr Oxford Don' by John Agard; THE WOMEN'S PRESS LTD for 'Nothing Said' by Brenda Agard; HUTCHINSON PUBLISHING GROUP LTD for 'Nature's Politics' by Benjamin Zephaniah taken from The Dread Affair; DIETER KLEIN ASSOCIATES for 'Girls Can We Educate We Dads?' by James Berry; REX COLLINGS LTD for 'Measure for Measure' and 'On Judgement Day' by Sipho Sepamla; VIRAGO PRESS LTD for 'Preacher, Don't Send Me' by Maya Angelou; METHUEN LONDON for 'Questions from a Worker Who Reads' by Bertolt Brecht trs. by Michael Hamburger; BLOODAXE BOOKS for 'Casualty' by Miroslav Holub trs. by Ewald Osers taken from Poems Before and After: Collected English Translations (1990) and 'Pencil Letter' and 'It's Not That I'm Scared' by Irina Ratushinskaya trs. by Richard McKane and Helen Szamuely taken from Pencil Letter (1988); DAVID HIGHAM ASSOCIATES for 'Florida Road Workers' by Langston Hughes taken from Selected Poems of Langston Hughes; 'Spic Take The Broom' © 1973 by Pedro Pietri. Reprinted by permission of MONTHLY REVIEW FOUNDATION;TERENCE LEE for 'Me Aunty Connie'; ALAN C. BROWNJOHN for 'Common Sense'; AMNESTY INTERNATIONAL PUBLICATIONS for 'Last Will and Testament' by Ariel Dorfman; HEINEMANN EDUCATIONAL for 'Cold' and 'Letter to Martha' by Dennis Brutus; AMY BARNARD for 'Pet Hates'; JULIA STUBBS for 'Women Are'; DAVID McWILLIAMS for 'Waiter! There's An Elephant In My Soup'; JUDITH PEEL for 'Thro' The Keyhole'; THEODORA CROW for 'A Feather Or a Hand'; AISLING HOGAN for 'A Shout In The Silence'; SALLY-ANNE CLARK for 'Hate'; MATTHEW DAVIES for 'Behind Closed Doors'; SADI HUSAIN for 'Not In India'; ALEX COLE for 'The Price of War'; PENGUIN BOOKS AUSTRALIA LTD for the untitled poem by Jeltje taken from Off The Record.

The Publishers have made every attempt to trace the copyright holders, but in cases where they may have failed will be pleased to make the necessary arrangements at the first opportunity.

We are also grateful to the following for permission to reproduce photographs:

AMNESTY INTERNATIONAL page 89; THE ANCIENT ART AND ARCHITECTURE COLLECTION 15; ASPECT PHOTO LIBRARY LTD 121 (M Wells); BARNABY'S PICTURE LIBRARY 19 (B Gibbs), 31, 116/ 117 (D A Simpson); JANE BROWN 46; BBC 11, 77, 84; J ALLAN CASH LTD 63; FORMAT PHOTOGRAPHERS 53 (V Wilmer); SALLY AND RICHARD GREENHILL 81; THE HULTON PICTURE COMPANY 36, 59, 61, 66; CRONID LUBARSKY 99; ROBERT OPIE COLLECTION 69; REX FEATURES LTD 49 (J Kuus); THE SUNDAY PEOPLE 110; THE TATE GALLERY, LONDON 17; UPI/BETTMANN 85; JANINE WIEDEL PHOTO LIBRARY 109, 115.

First published 1991
Second impression 1993

© The author and BBC Enterprises Limited/Longman Group UK Limited 1991
Book and cover design by Rob Green   Book and cover illustrations by Phyllis Mahon

Picture research by Helen Taylor

Published by BBC Educational Publishing and Longman Group UK Limited
BBC Educational Publishing, a division of
BBC Enterprises Limited
Woodlands
80 Wood Lane
London W12 0TT

Longman Group UK Limited
Longman House
Burnt Mill
Harlow
Essex CM20 2JE
England
and Associated Companies
throughout the World

ISBN 0 582 08550 0

Set in Perpetua
Typeset by Ace Filmsetting Ltd, Frome
Text printed in Singapore
Cover printed in Singapore